Where S
Go to Die

Mari Bolte

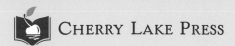
CHERRY LAKE PRESS

Published in the United States of America by Cherry Lake Publishing Group
Ann Arbor, Michigan
www.cherrylakepublishing.com

Reading Adviser: Beth Walker Gambro, MS, Ed., Reading Consultant, Yorkville, IL
Content Adviser: Robert S. Kowalczyk, MS, Physics, Systems Engineer (Retired) at the NASA Jet Propulsion Laboratory

Photo Credits: page 1: ©NASA, ESA, Joseph Olmsted (STScI)/hubblesite.org; page 5: ©MARK GARLICK/SCIENCE PHOTO LIBRARY/Getty Images; page 6: ©muratart/Shutterstock; page 9: ©Chris Gunn/nasa.gov; page 10: ©ESA/Webb, NASA & CSA, L. Armus, A. S. Evans/nasa.gov; page 12: ©MARK GARLICK/SCIENCE PHOTO LIBRARY/Getty Images; page 15: ©Hubble Legacy Archive, NASA, ESA/nasa.gov; page 16: ©NASA, ESA, CSA, and STScI/flickr.com; page 19: ©Hubble Heritage Team (STScI/AURA/NASA/ESA)/esahubble.org; page 20: ©NASA, ESA, CSA, and STScI/flickr.com; page 22: ©BEST-BACKGROUNDS/Shutterstock; page 23: ©Vadim Sadovski/Shutterstock; page 23: ©REDPIXEL.PL/Shutterstock; page 23: ©Catmando/Shutterstock; page 25: ©Universal History Archive/Contributor/Getty Images; page 26: ©NASA, ESA, CSA, STScI/flickr.com; page 28: ©ESA/Hubble & NASA/esahubble.org

Cherry Lake Press is an imprint of Cherry Lake Publishing Group.

Library of Congress Cataloging-in-Publication Data
Library of Congress Cataloging-in-Publication Data has been filed and is available at catalog.loc.gov.

ISBN 9781668938393 Lib.

Cherry Lake Publishing Group would like to acknowledge the work of the Partnership for 21st Century Learning, a Network of Battelle for Kids. Please visit Battelle for Kids online for more information.

Note from publisher: Websites change regularly, and their future contents are outside of our control. Supervise children when conducting any recommended online searches for extended learning opportunities.

Printed in the United States of America

Mari Bolte is an author and editor of children's books in every subject imaginable. She hopes the next generation sets their sights on the sky and beyond. Never stop the love of learning!

CONTENTS

Chapter 1
What Stars Leave Behind | 4

Chapter 2
The Brightest Black Hole | 8

Chapter 3
A Thousand Views | 14

Chapter 4
Stellar Circle of Life | 18

Chapter 5
Chaos in the Cartwheel Galaxy | 24

Activity | 30
Find Out More | 31
Glossary | 32
Index | 32

What Stars Leave Behind

Nothing can escape a **black hole**'s gravity—not even light. Space objects like stars, planets, and meteors can get too close. They are consumed. All of their matter and energy become part of the black hole. Objects can also keep a safe distance. They orbit black holes. The intense gravity stops them from flying away in all directions. Many black holes are born from the chaotic death of a star.

For many stars, the end of its life begins when its fuel runs out. The star collapses. Its core is compressed. This causes an explosion called a **supernova**. Part of the star is blasted into space. If the star is small, it becomes a **neutron star** or white dwarf star. If it is massive, it leaves a black hole.

As shown in this artist's representation, when a star gets too close, a black hole pulls it in. Its gravity shreds the star. The star's gases are devoured.

A black hole can't be seen like stars and other space objects. But scientists know that it's there. They can measure the **radiation** created by dust and gas being drawn in. They see how the black hole's gravity affects space around it. In April 2023, the *James Webb Space Telescope* found the oldest known black hole. It is 10 million times more massive than our Sun. Scientists believe it formed 570 million years after the **Big Bang**. Every day, facts are being revealed about where stars go to die and what they leave behind.

Black Hole Facts

Small black holes can move through space, powered by their SUPERNOVA EXPLOSION. There is one speeding up to 248,500 miles (about 400,000 kilometers) per hour through the Milky Way.

Black holes are very **dense**. Imagine shrinking our planet down to the size of a GOLF BALL. That golf ball would still be as massive as the full-sized planet.

There is a black hole at the center of the MILKY WAY GALAXY. Scientists believe there is a black hole at the center of every large galaxy.

CHAPTER 2

The Brightest Black Hole

If you live in the Northern Hemisphere, look to the night sky on a dark fall night. Pegasus is the seventh-largest constellation. Within it is a galaxy called NGC 7469. And inside NGC 7469 is a supermassive black hole. NGC 7469 is a spiral galaxy. It faces Earth flat and head-on. This makes it easier to see the black hole at its center. The black hole is surrounded by a ring of young stars.

In December 2022, *Webb* took an incredible image. A cloud of **space dust** swirls around a dark black background. The arms of a spiral galaxy can be clearly seen. Red-and-white glowing dots—other galaxies—are sprinkled across the sky. And NGC 7469 is at its exact center.

Webb can see things in great detail. This is because of its large mirror. It is the largest mirror ever launched into space.

Red rays seem to shoot out from the galaxy. They are called **diffraction** spikes. These are caused by light bending around the edges of *Webb*'s mirrors. All bright objects captured by *Webb* show the same eight-pointed spikes. *Webb*'s main mirror is made up of smaller, hexagon-shaped mirrors. Each of the six hexagonal sides produces a spike. Two smaller spikes are made as light bounces off a support piece.

NGC 7469 was
FIRST
DISCOVERED
in 1784.

Space dust is made
from elements like
HYDROGEN, IRON,
AND CARBON. The
elements are in molecules
that form into
dust particles.

NGC 7469 Facts

The galaxy is around 90,000 **light-years** across. It is around 220 MILLION LIGHT-YEARS away from Earth.

This artist's image shows the most powerful active galactic nuclei, called quasars.

There is an active galactic **nucleus** (AGN) around NGC 7469's black hole. This is an area full of light. The black hole pulls in dust and gas. This creates superbright radiation. The bright light helps the *James Webb* see distant objects. With its help, *Webb*'s **infrared** cameras can pierce thick layers of space dust.

The same space dust that surrounds the black hole is responsible for the birth of young stars. Stars need large amounts of gas and space dust to be born. A starburst ring wraps around NGC 7469's black hole. The ring lies 1,500 light-years away. In this area, young stars are formed at a fast rate.

This is not the first time a black hole has been seen playing a role in star birth. In 2019, the Chandra X-ray Observatory discovered a jet of energy. It stretched a million light-years long. That jet was traced back to a supermassive black hole. The jet created a shock wave across galaxies. The shock wave created new stars.

SEEING IN INFRARED

Everything gives off radiation. We can only see a small amount of that radiation, though. That's called visible light. Infrared light has longer **wavelengths**. We can't see it with just our eyes. But tools on the *James Webb Space Telescope*, like the Near-Infrared Camera (NIRCam), can.

As the universe expands, things move away from Earth quickly. Light stretches. The wavelengths get longer. Visible light is absorbed by clouds of space dust. And unfortunately, space dust usually gathers around things we want to see! However, NIRCam can pick up the infrared wavelengths. This means *Webb* can see through the dust. It can also see stars and galaxies that were once invisible to us.

Webb's other cameras can take images using different wavelengths. Using those tools, it can identify the light from stars and dust. Scientists combine all the images into one. They get a deeper view of what else is out there.

CHAPTER 3

A Thousand Views

There are billions of galaxies out there. Some we have only caught as glimpses. With every glimpse, we gain another piece of knowledge. In July 2022, the *James Webb Space Telescope* sent back an image of Stephan's Quintet. The image was more than a mere glimpse. It was a complex look at the death of galaxies. The photo shows five galaxies. Four are in the process of colliding. The top galaxy has an AGN at its center. The AGN is 24 million times more massive than our Sun. It is pulling in the other galaxies.

Four of the galaxies in the quintet are part of a compact galaxy group. The galaxies in a compact group are close together. They are separated by distances roughly equal to the sizes of the galaxies themselves. Galaxies in a loose group are spaced much farther apart.

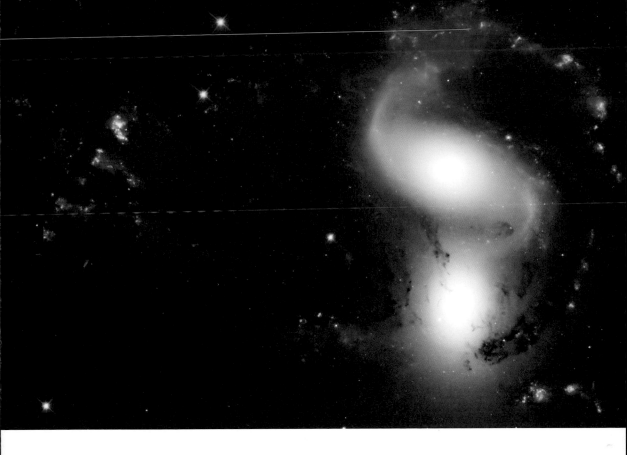

Stephan's Quintet was first discovered in 1877. It was not photographed until 2009.

You might think there are only four galaxies in *Webb*'s image. The central galaxy with the curving core is actually two galaxies. One of the galaxies, NGC 7318b, is cutting through the group. It's moving 2 million miles (3.2 million km) per hour.

Stephan's Quintet was the largest picture *Webb* had ever taken. It was created from nearly 1,000 separate image files. Having so many different images allows scientists to focus on certain details while looking at the same view.

Stephan's Quintet is also known as HICKSON COMPACT GROUP 92. It was first discovered in 1877.

Stephan's Quintet Facts

Scientists used to believe that COMPACT GROUPS were random. But recent discoveries have proven that gravity holds them together.

Quintet means "five," but only four galaxies are really part of the compact group. The FIFTH GALAXY, on the left, is only 40 million light-years away from Earth. The others are 290 million light-years away.

CHAPTER 4

Stellar Circle of Life

Stars are born inside clouds of space dust called nebulae. *Nebulae* means more than one nebula. Gravity pulls the **particles** into a mass. A process called nuclear **fusion** takes place. The mass becomes denser and hotter. Eventually, it becomes a star. Stars can live anywhere from 10 million to more than 12 billion years.

Eventually, though, the star runs out of fuel. The star's core is thrown off balance. It can no longer hold onto its outer layer of gases and dust. They are released and expand outward. Sometimes, they swallow nearby planets. The radiation from the star's core lights up the cloud. This glowing cloud is called a **planetary nebula**. The nebula is not related to planets. It got the name from the planetlike shape it forms. Eventually, the nebula breaks up, sending the space dust into space.

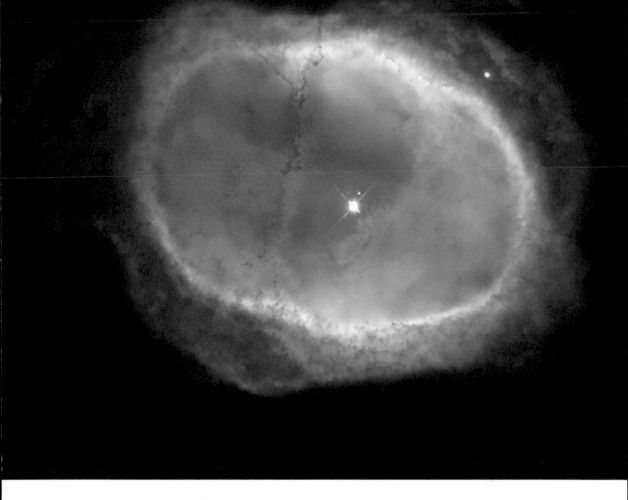

The star at the center of the Southern Ring Nebula has been sending out gas and space dust for thousands of years. This image was taken by *Hubble* in 1998.

The *James Webb Space Telescope* captured the stellar circle of life in action in July 2022. The Southern Ring Nebula is 2,500 light-years from Earth. NIRCam was able to see through the glowing cloud and into the nebula's center. A dead core, called a white dwarf, is all that's left of the original star.

Southern Ring Nebula Facts

Scientists believe that the Southern Ring Nebula's star was nearly THREE TIMES AS MASSIVE as our Sun.

The SOUTHERN RING NEBULA is 0.5 light-years across.

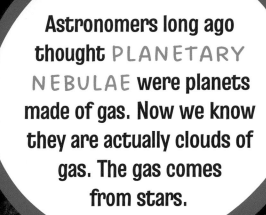

Astronomers long ago thought PLANETARY NEBULAE were planets made of gas. Now we know they are actually clouds of gas. The gas comes from stars.

A visible light telescope makes the Southern Ring Nebula show up in different colors.

The Southern Ring Nebula's white dwarf is bright and clear in *Webb*'s image. As many as five other stars helped shape the nebula. Scientists have compared different images taken by *Webb*'s cameras. These scientists are able to see jets of energy, orbits, and other places where the stars interact with each other.

Planetary nebulae do not stick around long. They last between a few thousand and 20,000 years. It sounds like a long time. However, this is just a short period of time in a star's life cycle. Astronomers have found around 20,000 planetary nebulae in the Milky Way so far. Only around 3,500 of them have been observed and cataloged. This is because there is space dust surrounding these planetary nebulae that hides them. But with *Webb*'s help, hopefully scientists will be able to study them all.

Invisible Mysteries

TYPES OF BLACK HOLES:

Stellar-mass Black Holes:

Stellar-mass black holes are the smallest type. They form when a star collapses into itself. They are between a few and 100 times more massive than the Sun. The Milky Way has anywhere from 10 million to 1 billion stellar-mass black holes.

Intermediate Black Holes:

Intermediate black holes are larger than stellar-mass black holes but smaller than supermassive black holes. Some scientists believe they form when multiple stellar-mass black holes combine. However, little is known about intermediate black holes. There may be as many as 46,000 in the Milky Way.

Supermassive Black Holes:

No one knows how supermassive black holes are made. With a mass between 100,000 and more than 60 billion times greater than our Sun, they are huge. There is one supermassive black hole at the center of the Milky Way.

CHAPTER 5

Chaos in the Cartwheel Galaxy

Around 400 million years ago, the Cartwheel Galaxy was a regular spiral galaxy. Then a smaller spiral galaxy plunged into it head-on. The resulting shock wave created a ring of material that blasted outward from the center of the Cartwheel Galaxy. The material settled in a circular starburst shape.

The smaller galaxy continued on its way and passed through. It dragged a trail of hot gas with it. The Cartwheel Galaxy was left forever changed.

A black hole sits at the Cartwheel Galaxy's center. The bright core is surrounded by a ring. Reddish-pink lines swirl around the core in the same direction.

The *Hubble Space Telescope* photographed the Cartwheel Galaxy and its companions in 2016.

The swirls are actually the remains of the galaxy's spiral arms. They stretch and connect it to the larger ring around the galaxy's edge. Both rings have been moving outward since the impact first happened, like ripples in a pond.

Cartwheel Galaxy Facts

The CARTWHEEL GALAXY has three companion galaxies. Two can be seen together here. The third is outside the scope of the image.

The Cartwheel Galaxy is **500 MILLION LIGHT-YEARS** away in the constellation Sculptor.

One **COMPANION GALAXY** resembles the Cartwheel Galaxy in color. Its red color comes from hydrocarbon-rich dust.

NGC 1566 is a grand design spiral galaxy. It is also known as the Spanish Dancer. Its spiral arms are easy to see.

There are many types of galaxies. The most common type is spiral. With curving arms, these galaxies look like pinwheels. Elliptical galaxies resemble stretched-out ovals. Irregular galaxies don't have a defined shape.

The Cartwheel Galaxy is a ring galaxy. Ring galaxies are unusual. Only 1 in 10,000 of all known galaxies are rings. The first was not discovered until 1950.

All ring galaxies have a dense central core. That core is usually made from old stars. It has little gas for making new stars. The space around the core is nearly empty. Then a dense collection of extremely bright stars makes up the outer ring. This means they are hot, young stars. This stretch of space is littered with supernovas as well.

Webb's powerful tools have let scientists study the Cartwheel Galaxy as never before. They are now able to see the full stellar life cycle in action and better understand where stars go to die.

A SUSPECTED SUPERNOVA

One of the first things *Webb* spotted when it got to work was a suspected supernova. Finding supernovas isn't part of *Webb*'s mission. Usually, telescopes that scan huge sections of the sky are given this job. But *Webb* was able to spot a bright object around 3 to 4 billion light-years away. Over 5 days, the light faded.

Scientists compared *Webb*'s photos to some taken previously by the *Hubble Space Telescope*. The burst of light was not in *Hubble*'s images. Scientists concluded the flash was from a supernova, caught by pure luck.

The star was probably a young star. It is hard to capture a supernova in action. The explosion lasts a fraction of a second. Then the nebula fades after a few days. *Webb* had made an amazing discovery.

Activity

Connect to STEAM: Science

Every day, NASA releases a picture of the day. The image or photograph is of something in our universe. Then a professional astronomer writes an explanation to go with it. With an adult's help, search the internet for "NASA Astronomy Picture of the Day."

Then take the next step and learn more about something in the image. Some ideas and questions you could ask include:

- What kind of star or planet was shown?

- What kind of camera was used to take the picture? Where was it located?

- Who took the image?

- How did the object pictured in the image get its name?

- Click one of the links in the explanation and read whatever pops up.

- Find out more about the constellation that was mentioned.

Share what you learn by making a poster display. Include the image you investigated and the most fascinating facts you learned.

Find Out More

Books

Bjazevich, Wendy. *Exoplanets: A Visual Guide to the Worlds Outside Our Solar System*. Fresno, CA: Bushel & Peck Books, 2023.

Bolte, Mari. *Earth vs. Mars*. Ann Arbor, MI: Cherry Lake Publishing, 2022.

Hirsch, Rebecca E. *Stars and Galaxies in Action: An Augmented Reality Experience*. Minneapolis: Lerner Publications, 2020.

Virts, Terry. *The Astronaut's Guide to Leaving the Planet*. New York: Workman Publishing Company, 2023.

Online Resources to Search with an Adult

European Space Agency: Black Holes for Kids

Here's the Journey Through an Exploded Star

National Geographic: Black Holes

ViewSpace

Glossary

Big Bang (BIG BAYNG) an explosion that scientists believe started the formation of the universe

black hole (BLAK HOHL) an invisible area with gravity so strong that space objects and light cannot escape its pull

dense (DENS) very thick and heavy

diffraction (di-FRAK-shuhn) when a beam of light is bent or spread out

fusion (FYOO-zhuhn) a reaction where two or more things are joined

infrared (in-fruh-RED) invisible light from beyond the red end of the visible light spectrum

light-years (LYTE-YEERZ) units of distance equal to how far light travels in 1 year—6 trillion miles (9.6 trillion km)

neutron star (NOO-trahn STAHR) the small, dense core of a collapsed large star

nucleus (NOO-klee-uhs) the central part of an object

particles (PAHR-tih-kuhlz) very small, basic units of matter

planetary nebula (PLA-nuh-teh-ree NEB-yoo-lah) a giant cloud of dust and gas, often called a "star nursery"

radiation (ray-dee-AY-shuhn) energy that comes from a source in the form of waves or rays you cannot see

space dust (SPAYS DUHST) tiny bits of matter from comets, asteroids, and other space objects that collect into clouds

supernova (soo-puhr-NOH-vuh) the explosion caused by the collapse of a star's core

wavelengths (WAYV-lengths) measurements between one wave to another as energy flows through space in a wavelike pattern

Index

active galactic nuclei (AGN), 12, 14

black holes, 4–8, 12–13, 23–24

Cartwheel Galaxy, 24–29

diffraction spikes, 9

Hickson Compact Group, 16
Hubble Space Telescope, 29

infrared light, 12–13

James Webb Space Telescope, 5, 8–9, 12–15, 19, 22, 29

Milky Way, 6, 7, 22–23

nebulae, 18–19, 21–22, 29
NGC 7469, 8–11
NIRCam, 13, 19

planetary nebulae, 18, 21–22

radiation, 5, 12–13, 18
ring, 28–29

Southern Ring Nebula, 19–20, 22
space dust, 5, 8, 10, 12–13, 18, 22, 27
spiral galaxies, 8, 24–25, 28
Stephan's Quintet, 14–16
supernovas, 4, 6, 29

visible light, 13